Media and Technology

by Imogene Forte and Sandra Schurr

Incentive Publications, Inc
Nashville, Tennessee

Cover Photos by Jerry R. Atnip
Cover Design by W. Paul Nance
Illustrated by Marta Drayton

ISBN 0-86530-377-0

Copyright ©1997 by Incentive Publications, Inc., Nashville, TN. All rights reserved. No part of this publication may be reproduced, stored in a retrieval system, or transmitted in any form or by any means (electronic, mechanical, photocopy, recording, or otherwise) without written permission from Incentive Publications, Inc., with the exception below.

Pages labeled with the statement ©1997 by Incentive Publications, Inc., Nashville, TN. are intended for reproduction. Permission is hereby granted to the purchaser of one copy of **MEDIA AND TECHNOLOGY** to reproduce these pages in sufficient quantities for meeting the purchaser's own classroom needs only.

PRINTED IN THE UNITED STATES OF AMERICA

TABLE OF CONTENTS

Preface 7
A Is for the A to Z of Media and Technology 9
    Brainstorming
B Is for Brains and Computers 10
    Read and Relate
B Is for Book-Talk Back Talk 12
    Interest Inventory
C Is for Camera Close-up Calendar 14
    Calendar Investigations
C Is for Computers 15
    Cooperative Learning: Think/Pair/Share
D Is for Databases 17
    Williams' Taxonomy
E Is for E-Mail 18
    Cooperative Learning (Jigsaw)
F Is for Fax Machines 22
    Bloom's Taxonomy
F Is for Film-Related Careers 24
    Research Activity
G Is for Graphics 25
    Bloom's Taxonomy
H Is for the History of the Computer 27
    Research Activity
I Is for Invasion of Privacy through Technology 30
    Direction Discussion
I Is for Investigating Mainframes 33
    Williams' Taxonomy
J Is for Juxtaposing Computer Concepts 35
    Short Writing Exercise
K Is for Knowing Computer Lingo 37
    Bloom's Taxonomy
L Is for Laserdisc 38
    Multiple Intelligences
M Is for Media Center 39
    Williams' Taxonomy
N Is for News and You 40
    Interview Exercise
O Is for Online 42
    Bloom's Taxonomy
P Is for Print Materials 44
    Research Activity
P Is for Printers and Printing 45
    Multiple Intelligences
Q Is for Questions on High Tech 46
    Research Activity

R Is for Researching Desktop Publishing 47
   Multiple Intelligences
S Is for Surfing the Net 48
   Discussion
T Is for Talk Shows 50
   Cooperative Learning
T Is for "Terminal" Disease 51
   Bloom's Taxonomy
U Is for Users 53
   Williams' Taxonomy
V Is for Virtual Reality 54
   Read and Relate
W Is for Word Processing 55
   Multiple Intelligences
X Is for eXamining Copyright 56
   Discussion
Y Is for Your Technology Attitude 59
   Learning Log
Z Is for Zest for Spreadsheets 60
   Read and Relate

Appendix

Planning a Schoolwide Media and Technology Fair 65

Student/Teacher/Business Planning Form 68

Suggested Authentic Assessment Measures

   Ten Possible Research Challenges 70

   Ten Possible Product Challenges 71

   Ten Possible Performance Challenges 72

   Ten Possible Methods to Test What I Know about Media and Technology 73

Journal-Writing Tasks Based on Myths Related to Technology 74

Journal-Writing Tasks Based on Myths Related to Media 75

Build Your Own Multimedia Technology Reference Bank 76

Using Investigation Cards
   to Smuggle Thinking Skills Into Classroom Instruction 77

PREFACE

From A to Z, *Media and Technology* presents high-interest activities to further student understandings, skills, and concepts related to the ever expanding world of media and technology. The collection of instructional tools, techniques, projects, and lessons has been designed to stretch the mind and increase problem-solving abilities while at the same time capturing and holding the students' interest and imagination.

Special features include activities:

- that use literature-based research for their design
- with established taxonomies and models for their organizational structure
- that focus on both directed and nondirected teaching methods for their delivery
- that provide options for both student reinforcement and enrichment

Teachers will find extensive use of Bloom's Taxonomy of Cognitive Development, Williams' Taxonomy of Creative Thought, and Gardner's Theory of Multiple Intelligences. Higher-order thinking skills and cooperative learning experiences have been infused throughout the book to add meaning and excitement to established media and technology curricula and/or exploratory and enrichment courses.

Finally, the book features a comprehensive appendix employing exemplary ideas, an overall plan for a schoolwide media and technology fair, journal entry starters and writing ideas, investigation cards, independent study topics, and authentic assessment measures including research challenges, product challenges, performance challenges, and test challenges.

In short, this book will provide the middle grades educator with a comprehensive resource featuring instructional and assessment strategies and techniques to integrate and enhance authentic instruction throughout the entire school year.

A IS FOR THE A to Z OF MEDIA AND TECHNOLOGY

BRAINSTORMING

A audiovisual, audiotape, animation, amplifier, artificial intelligence, access

B bit and byte, binary, bar code, bulletin board system, book, back up, bit map, bleed

C cellular phone, CPU, computer, CD-ROM, computer chip, cassette player, computer programmer, camera, camcorder, copyright law, computer crime, computer health, computer languages, cyberspace, cassette, clipboard

D data, disk, distance learning, digital image, disk drive, desktop publishing, disk capacity

E electronic, e-mail, electronic library/encyclopedia/dictionary, ethernet, encapsulated postscript (EPS)

F film, fax machine, film festival, fiber optic, flowchart, file, floppy disk, flight simulator, font

G graphics, graphic art

H hard drive, history of film, handshake

I Internet, input, information highway, icon, invasion of privacy, interface

J journalism, journal, journalist

K keyboard, knowledge, kilobyte

L lights/camera/action, laser, laptop, log-in name

M megabyte, movie, movie studio, micro/macro computer, media center, media specialist, magazine, mouse, monitor, modem, memory

N negative, network, newspaper

O output, overhead projector, opaque, on-line services, operating

P photography, programming, performances, projectors, personal computer, printer, public domain, postscript, prompt, port

Q quality performance, query

R radio, recording, remote control, robotic, reference, RAM, resolution

S software screen, script writing, spread sheet, satellite dish, sound/light waves, slides, scanners, studios, silicon chip, simulation

T television, telephone, telemarket, tape recorder, telecommunication

U understudy, user-friendly

V video, visual, video game, VCR, virus, virtual memory

W word processing, wavelength, World Wide Web, wildcard

X example, x-rays

Y "you name it"

Z zoom lens, zest for media and technology

©1997 by Incentive Publications, Inc., Nashville, TN.
Media & Technology

B IS FOR BRAINS AND COMPUTERS

READ AND RELATE

READ
Brains and computers work in similar ways. Your brain takes in information. A computer takes information you put in. The information that the computer takes in is called input.

RELATE
Draw a cartoon strip of a brain and a computer engaged in conversation with one another, talking about how they both know how to input information.

READ
Your brain remembers information. The computer remembers information so you can use it later. When the computer remembers information, it stores the information.

RELATE
Write down ten to twenty pieces of information currently stored in your brain (and that could be fed into a computer) that you would never want to forget.

READ
You can think about any information in your brain. The computer shows you information so you can decide what to do with it. When the computer shows you information, it displays the information.

RELATE
Compose a short story that gives as many explanations as you can think of for a computer that can no longer display information on its screen.

©1997 by Incentive Publications, Inc., Nashville, TN.
Media & Technology

B IS FOR BRAINS AND COMPUTERS cont.

READ
When you change your mind, the information in your brain changes. A computer changes the information when you want it to. For a computer to change information, you must edit the information.

RELATE
Tell about a personal experience you have had recently that caused you to change your mind or edit your ideas about a person, place, or thing.

READ
You give out information whenever you talk, write, or complete an action. A computer gives out information so you can share it with others. The information that the computer gives is called output.

RELATE
Give each letter of the alphabet a numerical code such as A = 5, B = 10, and C = 15. Use this number code to write a secret note on the computer as output and have a friend try to decipher your message from the display screen.

READ
Although people and computers are similar in many ways, computers do have three advantages over human beings when it comes to processing information. They can do the same job over and over again without getting bored. They can work more quickly than people. They can remember information for years without forgetting a single word, number, or fact.

RELATE
It has been said that computers may put schools out of business. Imagine that all schools in your community were closed and children were taught at home through the use of computers. Discuss with a group of peers what things would change. Which changes would make things better and which would make things worse?

B IS FOR BOOK-TALK BACK TALK

INTEREST INVENTORY

A question often asked in this age of high tech is, "Will books be replaced by modern technology?" Book lovers are usually quick to answer: "No! Never!" What do you think? Completing the "Book-Talk Back Talk" Interest Inventory will help you determine your answer.

It has been said, "A book can be the best of friends. It will go anywhere with you, and depending on your choice, will provide new insights and information, help you escape from or cope with reality, strain your brain, or stretch your imagination. Or it can be enjoyed just for enjoyment's sake."

To help you evaluate and understand your reading interests and habits, think about all the books you have read recently or hope to read in the near future.

1. The book I am reading now (or read last) is _____
   by _____ .

2. On a scale of 1 to 3, with 3 being the highest score, I would give this book a ____ .

3. When I evaluate a book's interest to me, I consider the following, in order numbered from 1 to 5.

   Plot ____

   Setting ____

   Characters ____

   Language ____

   Author's writing style ____

4. Right now I am especially interested in reading books about
   _____ .

5. The most beautiful picture book I've ever seen in my whole life is
   _____ .

B IS FOR BOOK-TALK BACK TALK cont.

6. I think our school library is _____.

7. I find our required reading to be

   challenging _____

   boring _____

   because _____.

8. The book I would choose to share with a person of my age from another country would be _____ by _____ because _____.

9. When evaluating my reading habits, I would say that for a person of my age I am a

   ( ) mature reader

   ( ) good reader

   ( ) exceptionally advanced reader

10. If I could take only one book on a long journey, I would take _____ by _____.

C IS FOR CAMERA CLOSE-UP CALENDAR

CALENDAR INVESTIGATIONS

☐ Examine a camera carefully. Locate and identify the major parts.	☐ Explain the function of each part of the camera.	☐ Write a brief explanation of how a camera takes pictures.	☐ Describe how a flash works.	☐ Describe how a light meter works.
☐ Why do photographers ask their subjects to say "cheese"? Think of three other words that would serve the same purpose.	☐ Use research materials to find out where and by whom the first camera was invented and used.	☐ Use a Venn Diagram to compare and contrast a camera and a camcorder.	☐ List ways that the human eye and a camera are alike and different.	☐ Make up a story about a magic camera that would only take pictures of happy scenes and events.
☐ Agree or disagree with this quote: "A picture is worth a thousand words."	☐ What special traits, other than patience, do you think a photographer needs?	☐ Discuss whether or not photography is as much an art form as landscape painting.	☐ Write a definitive role description for a "photojournalist."	☐ Find out what happens in a darkroom to turn exposed film into photographs.
☐ Consult catalogs offering cameras for sale. Note the prices and determine an average price.	☐ How do you think family photograph albums help to build bonds and hold families together?	☐ List six ways a camera could be used to make classroom activities more interesting.	☐ Design a super-camera of the future and write a catalog description for it.	☐ List ten ways your life would be different if there were no cameras in the world.

14

©1997 by Incentive Publications, Inc., Nashville, TN.
Media & Technology

C IS FOR COMPUTERS

COOPERATIVE LEARNING: THINK/PAIR/SHARE

DIRECTIONS

Record your own responses to each of the questions below. Then discuss these ideas with a partner and record something of interest that he or she shared for each of the questions. If time permits, you and your partner should share your combined ideas with another pair of students. Can you determine why "two, three, or four heads are better than one?"

QUESTION ONE

How are you like a computer?

My Thoughts: _____

_____

_____

My Partner's Thoughts: _____

_____

_____

QUESTION TWO

What jobs can computers do?

My Thoughts: _____

_____

_____

My Partner's Thoughts: _____

_____

_____

C IS FOR COMPUTERS cont.

QUESTION THREE

How do computers think and talk?

My Thoughts:
_____
_____

My Partner's Thoughts:
_____
_____

QUESTION FOUR

How do computers solve problems?

My Thoughts:
_____
_____

My Partner's Thoughts:
_____
_____

QUESTION FIVE

Are computers smarter than people? Why or why not?

My Thoughts:
_____
_____

My Partner's Thoughts:
_____
_____

©1997 by Incentive Publications, Inc., Nashville, TN.

Media & Technology

D IS FOR DATABASES

WILLIAMS' TAXONOMY

Fluency
A database is a collection of data, facts, statistics, or information. Sports scores in newspapers, words in dictionaries, and listings in address books are databases. In two minutes, write down as many different databases as you can think of.

Flexibility
A database program is just a computer version of the examples you listed. But because computers work so fast, they can make the information very easy to find and update. Add types of database ideas that you would like to have if you had access to a database program on a home computer.

Originality
Each fact in a database is a piece of information called a field. All the information about one item in a database is called a record. Think up the most unusual and unique database idea for the principal to have in your school. Justify your choice.

Elaboration
Databases take a great deal of time and energy to develop and make operational. Write out a short essay defending this process entitled, "The Means Justify the End."

Risk Taking
Think of database ideas that would not be of benefit to you personally.

Complexity
It has been said that databases are a threat to our privacy. Explain how this could be true.

Curiosity
Databases are used in lots of ways. Schools often keep report cards and attendance records on the computer. Libraries use a database to keep track of their books. Airlines use databases to schedule their flying reservations and ticket sales. Think of some questions you might like to ask a school, a library, or an airline about the use or misuse of their database information.

Imagination
Pretend you are in charge of creating a database for the next generation of students. Write down possible things you would want to keep track of for these yet-to-be-born kids.

©1997 by Incentive Publications, Inc., Nashville, TN.
Media & Technology

E IS FOR E-MAIL

COOPERATIVE LEARNING (JIGSAW)

DIRECTIONS

During the Jigsaw activity you will work in a group of six in order to learn something new about e-mail, and then teach this information to members of your home group. Follow these directions.

1. Assign a number from one through six to each member of your home group. Each student will list the members of his or her home group on his or her recording sheet.

2. With the help of your teacher, give each member of your group his or her corresponding paragraph describing some important aspect of e-mail. Don't let anyone see any paragraph but his or her own.

3. When the teacher gives you the signal, locate the other people in small home groups in your classroom who have a number the same as yours. Meet with them and together learn the information discussed in your paragraph so that each of you becomes an "expert" on its content. You may take notes on the Recording Sheet. The group should then decide on a strategy for teaching what you have learned to the other members of your home group.

4. Return to your home team and teach the information in your paragraph to all of the other team members. Learn the information presented by them in their assigned paragraphs as well.

E IS FOR E-MAIL
RECORDING SHEET

DATE: _____

HOME GROUP MEMBERS

STUDENT ONE _____

STUDENT TWO _____

STUDENT THREE _____

STUDENT FOUR _____

STUDENT FIVE _____

STUDENT SIX _____

DIRECTIONS TO STUDENT

Cut apart the paragraphs about e-mail. Give each section to the appropriate person in your group. Meet with the other students in the class who have the same number as you do and together learn the information discussed in the paragraph. Work with these same students to complete the follow-up task for your paragraph, and share the results with your home group as well.

E IS FOR E-MAIL cont.

STUDENT ONE

E-mail is the fastest, most efficient, and least expensive model of electronic communication in the world. The advantages of e-mail are:

1) it is as immediate as a phone call, but the other person doesn't have to be there to receive the message; 2) you can send an e-mail whenever you want and the recipient can respond whenever they want; 3) you can also attach files and communicate with hundreds of people with a single message.

TASK: As if for your local newspaper, design a simple classified advertisement that promotes the use of e-mail for the average home or business.

STUDENT TWO

With e-mail, you can send notes to friends or coworkers and send queries or requests to special addresses to receive information. You can even conduct classroom projects by gathering information, "talking" to an expert on a specific topic, or writing and receiving e-mail from keypads. You can even participate in group discussions on a specific topic because e-mail makes it possible to communicate with many people at the same time.

TASK: Generate a list of "experts" that you and your group might want to access through e-mail in order to learn something about a specific topic appropriate for a project in a special course or subject area.

STUDENT THREE

Anyone can use e-mail if they establish an account with an Internet service provider or a commercial on-line service. A special e-mail account and corresponding address makes it possible for people to send you e-mail messages. However, in order to send and receive e-mail you need to have an e-mail software program.

TASK: Write down a list of criteria that you might use when selecting an e-mail software program for student use in your classroom.

E IS FOR E-MAIL cont.

STUDENT FOUR

Every e-mail address has similar elements that are necessary in order for e-mail to be correctly routed to the recipient. The president's e-mail address, for example, is president@whitehouse.gov. The part of the address after the @ is called the domain name, which is the name of the host or computer that is connected to the Internet from which the recipient receives his or her e-mail. The domain also gives the zone designation telling what kind of host it is or where it is. Each part of the domain name is connected by "dots." In the president's e-mail address, the domain name is "whitehouse.gov" with "whitehouse" being the host and "gov" being the zone designation.

TASK: Work with a small group of peers to compose an e-mail message to send to the president of the United States. Send it if you can!

STUDENT FIVE

In the president's e-mail address (president@whitehouse.gov), the combination of letters in front of the "@" is called the user ID or username. Most e-mail users choose their own username, which is often limited to eleven characters (letters and/or numbers). The username is like a mailbox in a large post office. The domain name would be the post office. If a mistake is made in an e-mail address, it will be returned to the sender.

TASK: Compile a list of "mock" e-mail addresses for the members of your class. What usernames and domain names will you use?

STUDENT SIX

Every e-mail message has the same elements, regardless of the computer system from which it was sent. Each message has an area for entering the recipient's address, another for "cc" addresses (which are names of other people who will receive this same message), another for the subject of the message, and another for the body of the message.

TASK: Design a series of standardized e-mail forms or formats that could be used for various types of messages to and from students and faculty members in your school.

©1997 by Incentive Publications, Inc., Nashville, TN.
Media & Technology

F IS FOR FAX MACHINES

BLOOM'S TAXONOMY

KNOWLEDGE
Identify what the word **fax** means. Consider the word "facsimile" in your response.

APPLICATION
Write out a set of directions (or create a flow chart) for sending a fax message and then use those directions to send one.

ANALYSIS
It has been said that computers and e-mail are helping to create a "paperless society." Determine the advantages and disadvantages of this trend among businesses and other institutions.

COMPREHENSION
In your own words, discuss how fax machines are competing with services provided to businesses and other institutions, such as schools, by the United States Postal Service.

©1997 by Incentive Publications, Inc., Nashville, TN.
Media & Technology

F IS FOR FAX MACHINES cont.

SYNTHESIS

Bookstores are selling publications that contain a wide variety of fax forms for celebrating special occasions, sending special reminders, or writing special messages. Create some original fax forms that kids might use to send messages in the classroom or school.

EVALUATION

Rank order each of the following types of communication from the most effective to the least effective for different groups of people. Establish your criteria before determining the rankings.

a. face-to-face dialogue
b. telephone conversation
c. handwritten note or letter
d. typewritten note or letter
e. computer-generated letter
f. mass-produced letter
g. fax letter

F IS FOR FILM-RELATED CAREERS

RESEARCH ACTIVITY

Producer	Actor
Director	Photographer
Script Writer	Set Designer
Wardrober	Sound Engineer

Select the film-related career that interests you most from the box.

Use the study plan below to learn about the career. When your research is completed, write a detailed role description for the career; list the personal characteristics and talents needed; and give the advantages and disadvantages of choosing the career as a lifelong occupation.

Research Study Plan

Study Plan for Research _____
_____
_____
_____

Things I Need to Know _____
_____
_____
_____

Resources I Will Need _____
_____
_____
_____

To Organize My Information I Will _____
_____
_____
_____
_____

G IS FOR GRAPHICS

BLOOM'S TAXONOMY

KNOWLEDGE

Graphics can be letters, numbers, pictures, lines, boxes, graphs, borders, patterns, and many other types of decorative tools found on most graphics software programs. Draw a symbol or example to represent each of these graphic elements.

COMPREHENSION

Graphics programs come with their own pictures, called "clip art." Some of the newer graphics programs will let you draw your own artwork and save it in the computer. In your own words, describe these "paint and draw" programs.

APPLICATION

Use a "paint and draw" software program to create a picture on your computer screen. Then practice using each of the following tools to embellish your picture:

fill: This is a tool that helps you color a picture without going outside the lines.

spray: This is a tool that works like a can of spray paint because it leaves a fine mist of color wherever you aim it.

magnify: This is a tool that works like a magnifying glass, making a part of your picture so large that instead of solid color you see a group of dots called pixels.

erase: This is a tool that wipes out parts of your picture without spoiling other parts of the drawing.

line draw: This is a tool that helps you draw a straight line without a ruler.

G IS FOR GRAPHICS cont.

ANALYSIS

Compare and contrast artwork of similar topics generated by computer graphic programs with those generated by artists not using computer graphics programs. How are they alike and how are they different?

SYNTHESIS

Use a "paint and draw" program to create an original banner, greeting card, poster, stationery, award, or certificate.

EVALUATION

Some artists feel that computer graphics are an inferior art form because they are generated by artificial, software-programmed tools. Develop a set of arguments to support or negate this position.

H IS FOR HISTORY OF THE COMPUTER

RESEARCH ACTIVITY

DIRECTIONS

Although the computer is a fairly recent phenomenon, there were many different and important inventions that led up to its development. Research each of the following predecessors to the computer and write down what you think each one's major contribution to the evolution of computer technology might have been.

Stonehenge

_____
_____
_____
_____
_____
_____
_____
_____
_____

Abacus

_____
_____
_____
_____
_____
_____
_____
_____
_____
_____
_____

©1997 by Incentive Publications, Inc., Nashville, TN.
Media & Technology

H IS FOR HISTORY OF THE COMPUTER cont.

Pascal's Adding Machine
_____
_____
_____
_____

Leibnitz's Calculator
_____
_____
_____
_____

Jacquard Loom
_____
_____
_____
_____

Analytical Engine of Charles Babbage and Countess Lovelace
_____
_____
_____
_____

H IS FOR HISTORY OF THE COMPUTER cont.

Tabulating Machine of Herman Hollerith

_____
_____
_____
_____
_____
_____
_____

Bonus Question

Can you think of any other inventions that might have influenced the development of today's computer technology?

IS FOR INVASION OF PRIVACY THROUGH TECHNOLOGY

DIRECTED DISCUSSION

PURPOSE

To enlighten students on the technological invasion of one's privacy which enables big business to examine the individual buying habits of consumers.

PREPARATION

None

PROCEDURE

1. Discuss the concept of "telemarketing" with students and take an informal survey of students whose homes or families have been contacted by some company marketing their products or services via the telephone during the past week. Encourage student reactions to this type of selling. Point out to students that The Telephone Consumer Protection Act of 1991 forbids marketers from calling homes within 12 months of specifically being told not to. Companies who violate this law can be taken to court and sued for damages. Discuss how these ill-timed telemarketing calls can be extremely disturbing. Suggest that students keep a record of the telemarketers who contact their homes during a given period of time. Record the names of businesses engaging in this activity and tally the number of calls class members receive.

2. Discuss the following facts about marketing strategies in our country today as reported by Bruce Horovitz from *USA Today* and as reported in *The Denver Post* on December 25, 1995:

   a. Unknowingly, through things people do every day—get the car washed, go to the grocery store, order a sweater from a catalog—they leave electronic fingerprints that give marketers crucial information.

   b. Powerful computers and high-tech scanners now enable marketers to closely monitor how, where, and when you spend your money.

   c. The typical consumer is on at least 25 marketing databases. There are more than 15,000 specialized lists containing 2 billion consumer names—each representing a potential sale.

   d. Marketing databases no longer just record your name and address.

I IS FOR INVASION OF PRIVACY THROUGH TECHNOLOGY cont.

They can turn to specialized information-gatherers who know far more personal information about us, from our race and gender to religious beliefs and political views.

    e. *Marketing databases can rent a list of one million names for $85,000.*

3. Share the following tips for stopping junk calls and mail with your students. Encourage them to use this information to develop a flyer that can be distributed to parents and local taxpayers as a community service effort by the school.

To Stop Telemarketing Phone Calls

a. *Send your name, address, and phone number to the Direct Marketing Association's Telephone Preference Service, P.O. Box 9014, Farmingdale, NY 11735. Tell them you want to stop receiving junk phone calls.*

b. *Consider an unlisted phone number. This keeps your name off lists taken from directories.*

c. *Call your local phone company's business office and request that your listing be removed from directories.*

d. *Don't have your phone number printed on your checks.*

e. *Write these companies that compile street address directories and ask that your listing be removed: R.L. Polk and Co., List Compilation and Development, 6400 Monroe Blvd., Taylor, MI 48180 and R.H. Donnelley, 287 Bowman Ave., Purchase, NY 10577.*

f. *Avoid ordering products or services via 800 or 900 phone numbers. Most can capture your number.*

g. *Tell telemarketers who phone to put you on their "do not call" list. If they continue to phone, you can sue and recover up to $500.00 for each call.*

h. *To take action against a telemarketer who keeps calling, send a certified letter, return receipt requested, demanding to be placed on their "do not call" list. Keep a copy of the letter and log each call.*

i. *Seek the aid of a privacy organization. For $20.00, Private Citizen will add your name to a directory of consumers who don't want junk phone calls. Contact Private Citizen, P.O. Box 233, Naperville, IL 60566.*

I IS FOR INVASION OF PRIVACY THROUGH TECHNOLOGY cont.

To Stay off Mailing Lists

a. Send your name and address to Direct Marketing Association's Mail Preference Service, P.O. Box 9008, Farmingdale, NY 11735. Tell them you want to stop receiving catalogs and other junk mail.

b. Avoid filling out so-called "warranty" cards for new products. These are not required for product warranties, and they give marketers personal information about you.

c. Use a variation of your name (add a middle initial or slightly misspell your name) each time you subscribe to a magazine or apply for a credit card. You then will be able to track which company is selling your name to what firm, based on how your mail is addressed.

d. Avoid entering sweepstakes and contests. These names are sold again and again.

e. Check the "opt out" box on sign-up forms when you subscribe to any magazines or sign up for any credit card. This prohibits the company from selling your name and address.

f. Use a post office box or mail drop as your address.

g. Think twice before using a supermarket "club" card when buying groceries. Many chains compile data based on customer purchases and target shoppers based on buying habits.

Copyright 1995. USA TODAY. Reprinted with permission.

IS FOR INVESTIGATING MAINFRAMES

WILLIAMS' TAXONOMY

Fluency

Mainframes are the largest, fastest, and most expensive computers. They are so powerful that they can process millions of instructions per second and they can be used by over one hundred people at any given time. Mainframe users often have to type in a password before they can start work on their terminal. Pretend you are going to access a mainframe and need an appropriate password. In one minute, list as many passwords as possible that represent yourself.

Flexibility

Think of as many projects as you can for a mainframe computer. Categorize the projects on your list in some way.

Originality

The biggest and fastest mainframes are called supercomputers or "monsters" because it takes a mainframe 90 seconds to do the work which a fast PC could complete in 20 hours. Write an original story about the "Biggest and Fastest" monster computer in the world.

Elaboration

Debate this statement: Bigger is better when it comes to computers!

I IS FOR INVESTIGATING MAINFRAMES cont.

Risk Taking

Pretend you have been given the unpopular task of convincing a business to downsize the use and power of its computers. What arguments will you use to show this business that people, not technology, make a company successful?

Complexity

Missiles in wartime contain computers which guide them to their targets. They are loaded with electronic maps and can process information from satellites which tell them where they can and cannot go. They are extremely accurate in their targets. Explain how the multiple uses of monster computers have both benefited and harmed humanity.

Curiosity

Some mainframes are so large that they require a Data Processing Department to run them. There are usually four major divisions in this department. The operations people are keyboard operators who enter data, librarians who store data, database administrators who organize data, and maintenance engineers who look after the hardware. The programming people develop new applications software. The systems analysis people design new computer systems as older ones become outdated. The information people help those users who need assistance with software. Make a list of job-related questions you would like to ask the different people who work in each section.

Imagination

Dating services use mainframes to match people with their "ideal" partner or mate. Imagine that you have just been given data on the perfect sweetheart for you. Describe everything about him or her.

©1997 by Incentive Publications, Inc., Nashville, TN.
Media & Technology

J IS FOR JUXTAPOSING COMPUTER CONCEPTS

SHORT WRITING EXERCISE

DIRECTIONS

Compare and contrast each of the following computer concepts. List ways that they are alike and different.

1. **Compare and Contrast**

   . . . a bit and a byte.

   _____

   _____

   _____

2. **Compare and Contrast**

   . . . hypercard and hypertext.

   _____

   _____

   _____

3. **Compare and Contrast**

   . . . RAM and ROM.

   _____

   _____

   _____

4. **Compare and Contrast**

   . . . input and output.

   _____

   _____

   _____

©1997 by Incentive Publications, Inc., Nashville, TN.
Media & Technology

J IS FOR JUXTAPOSING COMPUTER CONCEPTS cont.

5. Compare and Contrast
   . . . a mouse and a trackball.

   _____
   _____
   _____

6. Compare and Contrast
   . . . hardware and software.

   _____
   _____
   _____

7. Compare and Contrast
   . . . CAI and CAD.

   _____
   _____
   _____

8. Compare and Contrast
   . . . a spreadsheet and a simulation.

   _____
   _____
   _____

K IS FOR KNOWING COMPUTER LINGO

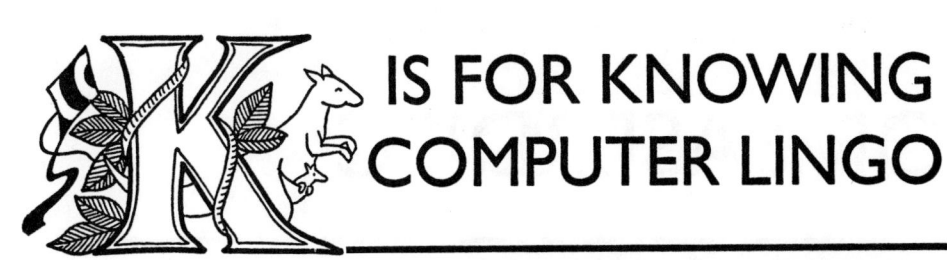

BLOOM'S TAXONOMY

KNOWLEDGE
Define these important computer terms: hardware, software, data, bits, bytes, RAM, ROM, disks, capacity, mouse, scanner, keyboard, program, cursor, printer, function keys, icons, input, output, and memory.

ANALYSIS
Compare and contrast the concept "virus" as it relates to computers and health care.

COMPREHENSION
In your own words, explain what it means to be "computer literate."

SYNTHESIS
Use any five of the words from the KNOWLEDGE Activity in an original paragraph about computers.

APPLICATION
Construct a crossword puzzle using the terms and definitions from the KNOWLEDGE activity.

EVALUATION
Determine which of the following computer-related terms would be most difficult to explain to someone not familiar with the computer world: Internet, Virtual Reality, Central Processing Unit, Desktop Publishing, or Information Technology.

©1997 by Incentive Publications, Inc., Nashville, TN.
Media & Technology

L IS FOR LASERDISC

MULTIPLE INTELLIGENCES

Verbal/Linguistic Intelligence

If you were explaining computer technology to a visitor from outer space in five sentences or less, how would you describe a laserdisc?

Logical/Mathematical Intelligence

Compare a laserdisc to a compact disc and a videotape.

Visual/Spatial Intelligence

Draw a simple picture or diagram of a bar code reader and a remote control for a laserdisc.

Body/Kinesthetic Intelligence

Train another student in laserdisc use and presentation.

Musical Intelligence

Act out a series of laserdisc images on a topic of your choice.

Interpersonal Intelligence

Work with a partner to write reviews about one or more laserdisc programs.

Intrapersonal Intelligence

Prepare a brief essay that tells others how the laserdisc could be an important tool for you in learning science or social studies.

M IS FOR MEDIA CENTER

WILLIAMS' TAXONOMY

Fluency
Think carefully about all the goods and services housed in your school media center. List as many as you can. Rank order these goods and services as to their value to you.

Flexibility
Using the ABC format, write as many words and phrases as you can that are related to your school media center.

Originality
Use the words and phrases from the Flexibility activity to design a word find or crossword puzzle for a friend to solve.

Elaboration
Debate this statement, "The book as a source of information will be completely replaced by technology within the next few years."

Risk Taking
Pretend you have been given the task of convincing a business in your community to contribute money for new computers and accompanying software for your local public school system.

Complexity
As school media centers have expanded to meet the needs of students growing up in a technology-dependent society, they have become more expensive and more complex in nature. Explain how this has influenced the overall school program. Take into account allotment of school funds for equipment training needed for media center directors, scheduling, and other concerns.

Curiosity
In your opinion, are all of the resources in your school media center used to the full advantage of both students and teachers? If not, are these resources underused because of scheduling or lack of access? Make a list of questions you would like to ask your teachers, fellow students, and the media center director about the benefits and unrealized potential benefits of the center. Compare your list with a classmate's list.

Imagination
Think about the changes that have been made in school media centers as they have expanded from all print material to include technology. Try to picture the changes that will be made in the next ten years as new and more efficient uses of technology are perfected. Write and illustrate a paragraph based on your vision.

©1997 by Incentive Publications, Inc., Nashville, TN.
Media & Technology

N IS FOR NEWS AND YOU

INTERVIEW EXERCISE

Use the "News and You" interview sheet to survey five members of your class. Find out how they learn about world news and how they apply it to their daily lives.

Then use the interview sheet to interview five adults in the twenty to thirty-five age range.

Next, use the interview sheet to interview five people in the thirty-five to fifty age range.

Finally, use the same interview sheet to interview five people over fifty.

Carefully compile the results of the four surveys.

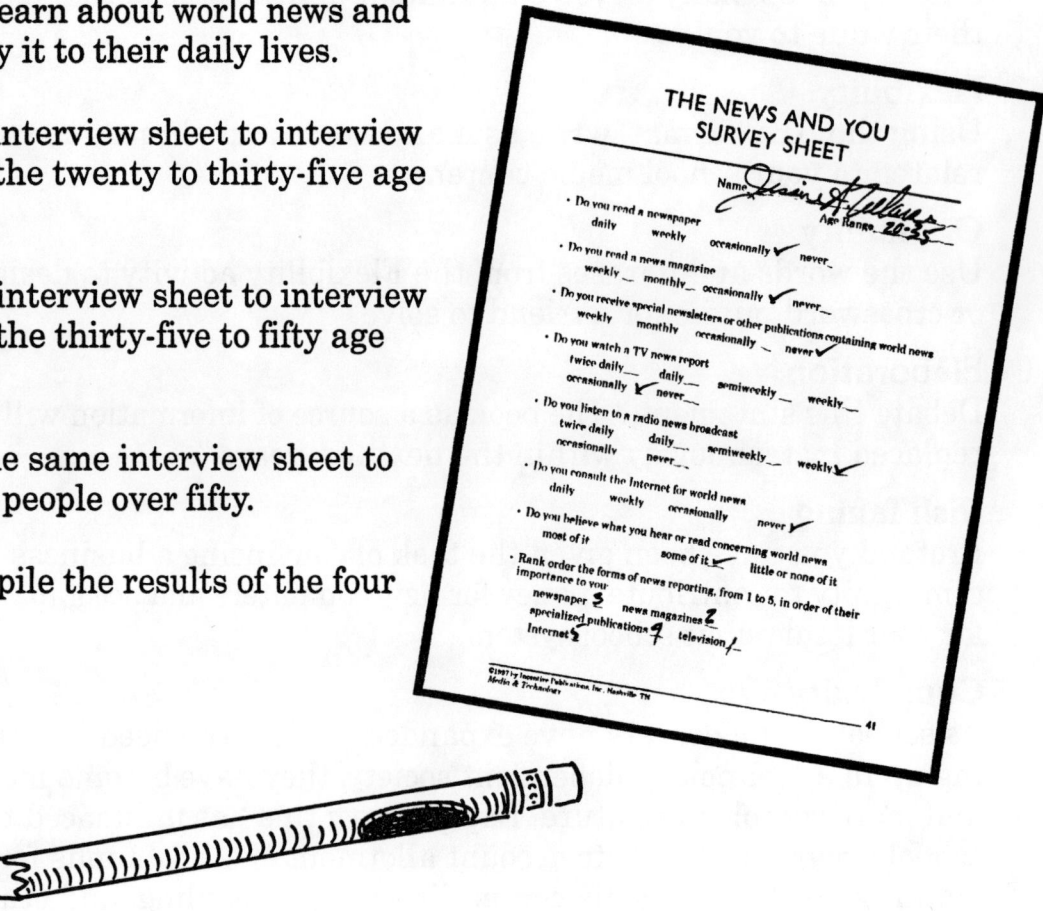

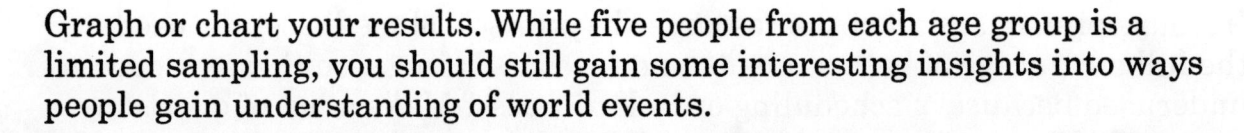

Graph or chart your results. While five people from each age group is a limited sampling, you should still gain some interesting insights into ways people gain understanding of world events.

Review the interview sheet carefully, and check each item as it relates to you, personally. Find out if your answers most nearly coincide with your own age group or that of another group. Could you predict how the acquisition and understanding of world news may affect hopes for world peace in the future?

©1997 by Incentive Publications, Inc., Nashville, TN.
Media & Technology

THE NEWS AND YOU SURVEY SHEET

Name_____

Age Range_____

- Do you read a newspaper

    daily___   weekly___   occasionally___   never___

- Do you read a news magazine

    weekly___   monthly___   occasionally___   never___

- Do you receive special newsletters or other publications containing world news

    weekly___   monthly___   occasionally___   never___

- Do you watch a TV news report

    twice daily___   daily___   semiweekly___   weekly___

    occasionally___   never___

- Do you listen to a radio news broadcast

    twice daily___   daily___   semiweekly___   weekly___

    occasionally___   never___

- Do you consult the Internet for world news

    daily___   weekly___   occasionally___   never___

- Do you believe what you hear or read concerning world news

    most of it___   some of it___   little or none of it___

- Rank order the forms of news reporting, from 1 to 5, in order of their importance to you:

    newspaper___   news magazines___

    specialized publications___   television___

    Internet___

41

©1997 by Incentive Publications, Inc., Nashville, TN.
Media & Technology

O IS FOR ONLINE

BLOOM'S TAXONOMY

KNOWLEDGE

We use the term "online" to mean "connected to another computer through a phone line." An online service is one that provides information and other features via that connection. Draw a graphic to show the meaning of "online" to another person.

COMPREHENSION

People go online for three reasons:

1. To do things faster and get information right away.
2. To reach more people (those known and those unknown) at once and more easily.
3. To do more with what is received because information from an online source is already in the computer for future use/reference.

Give three examples of something you might want to do online this very minute if you were connected.

APPLICATION

A person goes online for three reasons: to reach people, to get information, or to do one's work more effectively. To help you figure out how this might work for you at home or in the classroom, construct a chart with six columns (two for people, two for information, and two for work).

COLUMN ONE: People Who Are Already Important to Me

COLUMN TWO: People I Would Like to Connect With

COLUMN THREE: Kinds of Information That Are Important to Me Now

COLUMN FOUR: Kinds of Information I'd Like to Have

COLUMN FIVE: School/Homework I Do Now That Might Work Online

COLUMN SIX: School/Homework I'd Like to Try Online

O IS FOR ONLINE, cont.

ANALYSIS

Study the following list of things you can do online and decide which ones would be most useful to you in school or at home.

- conduct an interview
- talk with friends
- research a topic
- read a newspaper or magazine
- play a game
- send mail nationally or internationally
- get a phone number
- enter a contest
- discuss trivia
- write to an important person
- attend a support group
- provide a service
- hold a brainstorming session
- find stories about important people, places, or things

SYNTHESIS

Think up several unusual and unique passwords that you might choose to use when online. REMEMBER, HOWEVER, NEVER GIVE YOUR PASSWORD TO ANYONE!

EVALUATION

Determine how online activities could invade one's privacy, challenge one's security, or result in deviant or criminal behavior.

P IS FOR PRINT MATERIALS

RESEARCH ACTIVITY

Use this checklist as a guide for a treasure hunt to search out the "printed riches" of your school media center. As you locate printed materials devoted to each topic below, check it off on your checklist and remember where to find it next time you need it.

Atlas _____   Almanac _____   Autobiographies _____

Bibliographies _____   Biographies _____

Catalogs _____

Dictionaries _____

Encyclopedias _____   Economics _____

Fiction _____

Geography _____   Global Education _____

History _____   "How-to Books" _____   Health _____

Information Guides _____

Journalism _____   Jokes _____

Knowledge-Based References _____

Legends _____   Library Rules _____

Math _____   Maps _____   Magazines _____   Myths _____

Newspapers _____   Natural History _____   Novels _____

Organizational Guides _____

Posters _____   Picture Books _____   People _____   Poetry _____

Question and Answer Books _____

Recordings _____   Reader's Guides _____

Social studies _____   Sports _____   Short Stories _____   Science _____

Technical Manuals _____   Tall Tales _____

Universe _____

Values _____

Wellness _____   World Cultures _____

Your Own Personal Choice Books _____

Zoom In and Use These Treasures Now That You Know Their Exact Location _____

©1997 by Incentive Publications, Inc., Nashville, TN.
Media & Technology

P IS FOR PRINTERS AND PRINTING

MULTIPLE INTELLIGENCES

Verbal/Linguistic Intelligence
Write a brief description of a laser printer and a dot matrix printer.

Logical/Mathematical Intelligence
Compare and contrast how a laser printer works with how a dot matrix printer works.

Visual/Spatial Intelligence
Draw a set of cutaway diagrams to show how a printer prints.

Body/Kinesthetic Intelligence
The electronic scoreboard at a basketball game is a good example of dot matrix. Each score shows up as a pattern of dots. The windows that show the scores are set up like dot matrix print heads, but instead of pins, they have lights. The lights are arranged in eight columns and different numbers require the use of different columns. Draw a series of pictures to demonstrate this dot matrix application using varied numbers in your illustrations.

Musical Intelligence
Design a musical jingle to sell printers, making certain that the advertising message describes the differences in cost and performance of the two options.

Interpersonal Intelligence
Work with a friend to use the dot matrix concept as a springboard for creating a set of hidden messages for others to decipher. Hint: The format of a scantron sheet might get you started.

   OR

Considering the characteristics of a laser printer and a dot matrix printer, which one is most like you? Give reasons for your choice.

Intrapersonal Intelligence
Discuss the benefits of a laser printer over a dot matrix printer (or vice versa) with a friend.

©1997 by Incentive Publications, Inc., Nashville, TN.
Media & Technology

Q IS FOR QUESTIONS ON HIGH TECH

RESEARCH ACTIVITY

DIRECTIONS

Use the set of questions below to conduct some research about adults in your local school, neighborhood, or community to determine their "comfort zone" and use of personal computers in their lives. Compile your results in chart or graph form.

1. Do you own a computer?
2. Do you have any plans to buy a computer or upgrade your present computer?
3. How often do you use your computer?
    a. every day _____
    b. a few times a week _____
    c. few times a month _____
4. What do you primarily use your computer for?
    a. personal word processing _____
    b. personal/household budgets/spreadsheets _____
    c. professional use or home-based business _____
    d. personal files and/or games _____
    e. work brought home from the office _____
5. Do you use an online service? Why or why not? _____
6. If so, how often do you go online?
    a. every day _____
    b. a few times a week _____
    c. a few times a month _____
    d. a few times a year _____
7. Online, what are your primary activities?
    a. research/downloading information _____
    b. discussion groups/chat rooms _____
    c. e-mail _____
    d. lurking _____
    e. games _____

©1997 by Incentive Publications, Inc., Nashville, TN.
Media & Technology

R IS FOR RESEARCHING DESKTOP PUBLISHING

MULTIPLE INTELLIGENCES

Verbal/Linguistic Intelligence
In your own words, explain the concept, purpose, and process of desktop publishing (DTP).

Logical/Mathematical Intelligence
Most newspapers and magazines today are created with desktop publishing software packages. Desktop publishing is quicker and cheaper than methods that those used in the past. Compare and contrast an old method of publishing a newspaper page with the modern DTP method of publishing a newspaper page.

Visual/Spatial Intelligence
A desktop publishing program can produce text in many different styles of lettering, called fonts, and in different point sizes. Designers can then try out varied fonts and graphics to make their copy look nice and interesting. Create a series of different layouts for a project using the fonts as the basis for the varied layouts. Select those you like the best and be prepared to defend your choices.

Body/Kinesthetic Intelligence
Locate a desktop publishing software program and use it to print several letters in different fonts and point sizes.

Musical Intelligence
Create a set of rhythmic patterns to represent various fonts found on a popular desktop publishing program.

Interpersonal Intelligence
Using a desktop publishing program, create a newsletter to send to your friends. Tell about your school, hobbies, and recent activities. Include news about your friends, too. This is an especially good way to keep up with a group of long-distance friends.

Intrapersonal Intelligence
Use a desktop publishing program to print out your name in a variety of point sizes and fonts. Make a collage of your name with these designs.

S IS FOR SURFING THE NET

DISCUSSION

DIRECTIONS

Cyberspace is a kind of unsupervised playground. Some people you will meet on the Internet are not nice individuals. It is important to follow a set of rules when using the Internet just as you should follow rules when using playground facilities. Below are some suggested commonsense rules for kids and adults to observe. Discuss the reasons for each rule.

RULE ONE

Never give out personal information about yourself.

RULE TWO

Avoid unpleasant messages by ignoring them.

RULE THREE

Always be yourself and don't pretend to be somebody else who is older, wiser, or of another gender.

RULE FOUR

Make a budget and stick to it because being online costs time and money.

RULE FIVE

Express yourself honestly, but don't be accused of "flaming" (picking a fight).

RULE SIX

It's all right to be a "newbie" as you are learning to use the Internet, so don't be afraid to ask questions or make mistakes.

S IS FOR SURFING THE NET cont.

RULE SEVEN

Use your common sense to sort out good answers to your inquiries from wrong or inappropriate answers that you receive to your questions.

RULE EIGHT

Remember that online people are real people, so don't insult the person who is behind that remote keyboard.

RULE NINE

Share ideas, files, and yourself by posting messages and/or through the use of freeware.

RULE TEN

Cyberspace can be whatever you want it to be, so do what you can to make it a safe information and networking source.

T IS FOR TALK SHOWS

COOPERATIVE LEARNING

PURPOSE
To give students practice in conducting radio or television interviews using a talk-show format.

PREPARATION
Tape or purchase an episode of a popular television talk show or assign students to view a talk show prior to this activity.

PROCEDURE
1. Use the talk-show example as a springboard for discussing different ways people are interviewed on television and the different styles of talk-show celebrities conducting the interviews. Generate a class list of qualities that make for a good interview session.

2. Encourage students to plan and prepare a "Talk Show for Kids by Kids." Divide students into small cooperative learning groups of four to six students. Have each group develop a comprehensive outline for a new show that includes ideas for each of the following components:

    a. Name, time, and station/channel for talk show

    b. Format and brief description of talk show

    c. Suggested hosts/hostesses for talk show (including members of their group)

    d. Special guests to be invited and interviewed on talk show

    e. Special features of talk show

    f. Suggested sponsors (products or services) for talk show

    g. Special promotional activities for talk show

3. Instruct each cooperative learning group to put on a presentation showcasing their talk-show design for the other members of the class. Have students vote on the best talk-show plan and encourage the winning team to carry out their plans and actually stage an opening show.

©1997 by Incentive Publications, Inc., Nashville, TN.
Media & Technology

T IS FOR "TERMINAL" DISEASE

BLOOM'S TAXONOMY

KNOWLEDGE

1. Record facts you know about the computer.
2. Write down reasons why many people view computers as the enemy.
3. List ways computers can be useful to people who know how to use them.

APPLICATION

1. Collect and organize information about individuals who are said to be "techies."
2. Develop a plan to help people you know overcome their imaginary bouts with "terminal" illness.
3. Outline ways one could convince others that computers are indeed allies.

COMPREHENSION

1. Explain what you think is meant by the term "technophobia."
2. Describe some possible characteristics of a "technophobe."
3. Summarize some arguments that might be expressed by a "technophobe."

ANALYSIS

1. Determine the most basic reasons why people dislike "e-mail" and "voice mail" options for communicating.
2. Discover reasons why people have historically feared or avoided "hulking machines."
3. Debate this position: "Technophobia can be treated just like any other fear."

©1997 by Incentive Publications, Inc., Nashville, TN.
Media & Technology

T IS FOR "TERMINAL DISEASE" cont.

SYNTHESIS

1. Design a get-well card for someone suffering from "terminal" illness or "technophobia."

2. Write a short play or skit whose title reads: "Why Technology Bytes!"

3. Create a humorous glossary of common computer terms with different meanings for each term as spoken by a "technophobe" and by a "techie."

EXAMPLE:

Term: software

Techie Definition: a programming tool for computer use

Technophobe Definition: square flying discs

EVALUATION

1. Support or negate this statement made by Dr. Joyce Brothers, psychologist: "Human beings are meant to contact other human beings. And we're terrified machines will one day replace us."

2. Provide arguments, statistics, or other types of evidence for this position: "The best way to gain expertise and confidence with computers is to 'fool around with them.'"

3. Justify a new course for your school entitled: "Technophobia Recovery Program."

U IS FOR USERS

WILLIAMS' TAXONOMY

Fluency
List as many uses as you can think of for the computer today.

Flexibility
Classify your Fluency list of uses according to these three categories: **home, school, workplace.**

Originality
What is the most unusual and unique use of the computer you can think of for the home, the school, or the workplace?

Elaboration
Defend or negate this statement: "The use of the computer can improve a student's achievement level in school, the efficiency of parents/guardians in the home, and the performance of workers in the business world."

Risk Taking
Describe the most important thing for you to understand and appreciate when learning about or using the computer.

Complexity
Determine what is meant by the concept "user friendly" when it refers to the world of computers.

Curiosity
Make a list of questions you would be curious to ask someone who refused to learn how to use the computer.

Imagination
Visualize what life would be like if everyone in the world knew how to use the computer effectively.

V IS FOR VIRTUAL REALITY

READ AND RELATE

READ
Virtual reality is a concept that allows a person to create a world that doesn't really exist. When you watch television, it's as if you were looking through a window, but with virtual reality one can actually feel a part of the picture itself.

RELATE
Describe a world that you would like to create but that doesn't exist in your realm of experience.

READ
Flight simulators are virtual reality systems used for training airline pilots. A prospective trainee sits in a cockpit and a virtual reality scene is projected onto the windshield. The controls inside the cockpit are linked to a computer which alters the view and tilts and turns the cockpit as the trainee tries to fly the make-believe airplane. It feels, however, as if one is really flying in a real aircraft.

RELATE
Draw a picture of a situation that a trainee might have to simulate while learning to fly an airplane.

READ
A virtual reality system is being developed which allows a surgeon in one part of the world to operate on a patient thousands of miles away. Satellites transmit a life-size video display of the patient, and the surgeon performs the operation using a set of computerized hand controllers. A robot is programmed to follow the surgeon's hand movements precisely.

RELATE
Role play a situation where a surgeon is making a long distance telephone call to a prospective patient on the other side of the world, trying to convince him to have this "robotic" type of surgery.

©1997 by Incentive Publications, Inc., Nashville, TN.
Media & Technology

W IS FOR WORD PROCESSING

MULTIPLE INTELLIGENCES

Verbal/Linguistic Intelligence
Locate and write a review about a favorite piece of word processing software that is designed for kids to use.

Logical/Mathematical Intelligence
Compare and contrast two different word processing programs for kids.

Visual/Spatial Intelligence
Create a mini-poster promoting your favorite piece of software for word processing.

Body/Kinesthetic Intelligence
Demonstrate how to use a word processing program that is popular with students.

Musical Intelligence
Determine how musical clues or cues might enhance a word processing program.

Interpersonal Intelligence
Work with a partner to make a list of the many different ways a word processor could help a student to do his or her homework assignments more efficiently and more creatively.

Intrapersonal Intelligence
Use a word processing program to write about yourself.

X IS FOR eXAMINING COPYRIGHT

DISCUSSION

1. DID YOU KNOW

. . . that there are special copyright laws which regulate both the video and the computer industries? Write down two reasons why you think this is so.

REASON 1: _____
_____
_____
_____
_____

REASON 2: _____
_____
_____
_____
_____

2. DID YOU KNOW

. . . that when you purchase a video or piece of software for the classroom, you also buy the right to use it under reasonable circumstances? Explain what you think is meant by reasonable circumstances.

EXPLANATION: _____
_____
_____
_____
_____
_____
_____

©1997 by Incentive Publications, Inc., Nashville, TN.
Media & Technology

X IS FOR eXAMINING COPYRIGHT cont.

3. DID YOU KNOW

. . . that if you tape something from the television at home, in most cases you may not show it to a group other than your own family. Give two examples of when you might want to show a taped program to an outside group or crowd.

EXAMPLE 1: _____
_____
_____
_____
_____

EXAMPLE 2: _____
_____
_____
_____
_____

4. There are two exemptions possible for the situation in number three above. In a Face-to-Face Exemption, you can show the taped video to a group of students, providing you personally show it (and not someone else), and providing you erase it in a reasonable period of time. On the other hand, the Fair-Use Exemption allows you to use small portions of the video as long as it is part of a greater product, such as a montage of different television shows. Briefly describe a montage project of varied television programs that you might like to prepare for a project.

DESCRIPTION: _____
_____
_____
_____
_____
_____
_____
_____
_____

X IS FOR eXAMINING COPYRIGHT cont.

5. Software programs cannot be copied for any purpose other than for one backup copy. Justify this basic law for protecting companies from a pirated software problem.

JUSTIFICATION: _____

Y IS FOR YOUR TECHNOLOGY ATTITUDE

LEARNING LOG

DIRECTIONS

Respond to each of the following questions in your learning log. Take time to think through your ideas before recording them on paper.

1. Which of the following statements best describes your attitude towards computers and why?

   a. Computers are a modern convenience that everyone should have in their home and office for daily use.

   b. Computers are tools only for a select few who have highly technical jobs or interests.

   _____
   _____
   _____
   _____
   _____
   _____

2. Are you more like a CD-ROM, a fax machine, a laser video, a VCR, or a copy machine? Explain.

   _____
   _____
   _____
   _____
   _____

3. How would you argue for or against this position: "All students have an equal opportunity to learn computer skills in schools today."

   _____
   _____
   _____
   _____
   _____

©1997 by Incentive Publications, Inc., Nashville, TN.
Media & Technology

Z IS FOR ZEST FOR SPREADSHEETS

READ AND RELATE

READ

A spreadsheet is a computer software tool used to help compile and analyze numerical data. Spreadsheets allow the user to do basic number operations, to use formulas to study information, and to construct charts or graphs. In short, spreadsheets are most often used to make budgets.

RELATE

Construct a hypothetical budget for yourself over the next month. Plan creative ways that you might earn money and determine in advance how much money you will save and spend. Be specific in your plan.

READ

A spreadsheet program uses a worksheet to organize data. The worksheet is made up of columns that go up and down and rows that go across. When the columns and rows are placed on top of each other, a grid is formed. Each box in the grid is referred to as a cell. A worksheet grid can have many columns and rows. The size of the spreadsheet depends on the amount of numerical data you have to analyze.

RELATE

Redesign your hypothetical budget, if possible, using a spreadsheet software program. If this is not possible, construct a grid or spreadsheet manually for this task.

Z IS FOR ZEST FOR SPREADSHEETS cont.

READ

Most often, the grid labels the columns by capital letters and the rows by numbers. The cell address of the spreadsheet tells you which cell you are working with. It is made up of the column letter and the row number put together such as A6 or C26. When using a spreadsheet, the user puts words and numerals into the cells of the worksheet. Words are called labels and numerals are called values. The labels tell you what the values mean.

RELATE

Complete your hypothetical budget using either the spreadsheet software or inputting the data by hand.

READ

The power and appeal of spreadsheets is being able to ask "What if?" questions. Formulas make it possible to change one value in order to see the effect on all the other values.

RELATE

Pose a series of "What if" questions about your numerical data and see what effect these have on the figures. Some possible questions might be:

    What if I saved twice as many dollars as I spent this month?

    What if I increased my earnings by 10 percent?

    What if I spent $1.00 less on all my major purchases?

APPENDIX

PLANNING A SCHOOLWIDE MEDIA AND TECHNOLOGY FAIR

PURPOSE

A very effective culminating activity for a unit on media and technology would be a class or schoolwide fair to celebrate the wonders of technology and the tools of modern media. This fair could serve the school's community of students, teachers, and parents in such a way as to inform, to entertain, to instruct, and to market the unique contributions of the emerging Information Age. The steps for planning and implementing this event are outlined below.

Step One

Decide on a date, time, and place for the fair. Consider an evening time to accommodate working parents. Perhaps tie it in with a regularly scheduled meeting such as an open house, a parent-teacher association meeting, or a parent conference week. Consider using all key areas of your school facility, including indoor spaces such as classrooms, hallways, media center, and cafeteria as well as outdoor spaces such as playground fields and parking lots. Consider a popular time of the year for the fair, such as early fall to establish a community learning climate, a holiday season to establish a festive mood, or a late spring evening to commemorate the ending of a school year.

Step Two

Decide on a Fair Steering Committee to plan and coordinate the activities. Include student, teacher, administrative, and parent representatives on your committee. You might also want to include business representatives on this committee who are in the technology or media market in order to enlist their support, expertise, and resources. Several subcommittees might also be formed to include such responsibilities as:

PLANNING A SCHOOLWIDE MEDIA AND TECHNOLOGY FAIR cont.

1. Invitation and Public Relations Committee to determine the invitation design and the methods for advertising the fair throughout the school community

2. Booth and Exhibit Committee to determine the structure, theme, and organizational plan for the various functions and activities of the fair

3. Refreshment Committee to determine what food and beverages will be served and at what cost

4. Set Up Committee to determine the people power and methods required to get the fair up and running on the appointed day and at the designated time

5. Clean Up Committee to determine the people power and methods required to take down the fair booths and exhibits as well as to clean up the fair grounds and spaces

6. Host and Hostess Committee to determine who will greet the guests and serve as guides for the fair's special events and attractions

7. Budget Committee to determine the funding sources for the fair and to monitor all costs, expenses, and/or profits

8. Evaluation Committee to determine what assessment measures will be used to obtain feedback on the fair's success and/or problem areas

Step Three

Decide on a format and program for the fair. Consider such options as:

1. Student, teacher, and business exhibits of technology and media projects

2. Student, teacher, and business demonstrations of technology and media tools and techniques

3. Student, teacher, and business performances of technology and media-related concepts

4. Opportunities for guests to experiment with various technology and media-related equipment and software

PLANNING A SCHOOLWIDE MEDIA AND TECHNOLOGY FAIR cont.

5. Ongoing panels of students, teachers, and business people discussing topics and issues related to the changing world of technology and media

6. Public forums to exchange the mutual concerns, questions, and areas of expertise as it relates to technology and media

7. Special events such as technology and media-related skits, shows, role plays, case studies, and contests

Step Four

Decide on any follow-up steps or procedures to be conducted after the fair as well as ways to record or document the entire fair planning and implementation process for future reference.

STUDENT/TEACHER/BUSINESS PLANNING FORM FOR MEDIA AND TECHNOLOGY FAIR

Name_____ Date of Proposal _____

Type of Fair Activity or Event (check one)

_____ Exhibit

_____ Project

_____ Performance

_____ Demonstration

_____ Panel

_____ Forum

_____ Special event

_____ Other (please specify) _____

Learning Goals for the Project

_____
_____
_____
_____
_____
_____

Brief Description of Fair Activity or Event

_____
_____
_____
_____
_____

©1997 by Incentive Publications, Inc., Nashville, TN.
Media & Technology

STUDENT/TEACHER/BUSINESS PLANNING FORM cont.

Brief Description of Special Assistance or Resources I Will Need

_____
_____
_____
_____
_____
_____
_____

Brief Description of Expected Costs or Expenses

_____
_____
_____
_____
_____
_____
_____

Brief Description of Space, Equipment, or Facility Needs

_____
_____
_____
_____
_____
_____
_____
_____

©1997 by Incentive Publications, Inc., Nashville, TN.
Media & Technology

SUGGESTED AUTHENTIC ASSESSMENT MEASURES

Ten Possible Research Challenges

1. Do some research to find out how computer and media technology have changed over the years from your parents' generation to your generation. Predict what changes will occur during your generation.

2. Research to determine how databases have impacted our lives, both positively and negatively. Try to give specific examples to support your findings.

3. Research to discover the many exciting things one can do through the Internet and the World Wide Web. Rank order their importance or appeal to you.

4. Research to discover just how many adults and businesses work out of "electronic cottages." Determine what types of people and work lend themselves to this type of workplace organizational pattern.

5. Research to determine what types of software are the best learning tools for kids. Establish a rating scale for judging software based on your readings.

6. Research to uncover why some people are computer addicts while others harbor computer phobias. Try to construct a personality profile for each one.

7. Research to compare and contrast the "school library of yesterday" with the "school media center of today." Use a Before and After format for recording your ideas.

8. Research to deduce how advances in technology and media have influenced the world of advertising and marketing for consumer products. Use some specific data to support your findings.

9. Research to validate how technology and media have influenced (for better or worse) the home and family environment. What evidence or cautions might you pass on to your families?

10. Research to conclude how media and technology have either simplified or complicated our lifestyles today. Be able to defend your position.

©1997 by Incentive Publications, Inc., Nashville, TN.
Media & Technology

SUGGESTED AUTHENTIC ASSESSMENT MEASURES cont.

Ten Possible Product Challenges

1. Design a kid's page for the Internet.

2. Construct a student or parent guide for maximizing the tools and resources of your school or community media center/library.

3. Create a plan for weaning members of your family from their overdependence on the technology found in your home (such as television, video games, computers, etc.).

4. Write an essay to show ways that media and technology can enhance one's creativity.

5. Use a piece of software to write a story, compose a song, draw a picture, or solve a problem.

6. Compile a scrapbook of relevant media and technology newspaper and magazine articles.

7. Prepare a consumer guide for "young technology buffs" in your school who want to get the most for their money when purchasing technology-related products and services.

8. Plan and create a weekly or monthly newsletter on the theme of media and technology. Include factual or statistical information, charts or graphs, jokes or riddles, reviews or interviews, and bibliographies or summaries of software or publications.

9. Compile a directory of computer- and media-related careers that might be of interest to you and your peers.

10. Prepare a set of diagrams to show one or more of the following concepts.
    - How a camcorder works
    - How a fax machine transmits messages
    - How a laserdisc transfers images
    - How e-mail functions

SUGGESTED AUTHENTIC ASSESSMENT MEASURES cont.

Ten Possible Performance Challenges

1. Organize a computer or technology club for your school or neighborhood.

2. Conduct and tape an interview with a "computer whiz" in your school or community.

3. Prepare a technology quiz for kids and parents on concepts they should know. Administer the quiz to twenty people and give an oral report to summarize your results.

4. Write and deliver a "mini-lecture" on the blackboard or large piece of chart paper to report on a topic related to media and technology.

5. Stage a debate about the pros and cons of "surfing the net" without a set of guidelines, budget allocations, or monitoring devices.

6. Demonstrate your proficiency on a word processor for a friend.

7. Organize and moderate a panel discussion to help others understand more about the multiple uses of technology in the world today.

8. Create a set of puppets and a skit to teach preschoolers more about the wonders of technology.

9. Be prepared to criticize or defend this statement: electronic games inhibit the development of interactive communication skills among kids.

10. Produce and narrate a photo essay on how media and technology have influenced our everyday lives in this generation.

SUGGESTED AUTHENTIC ASSESSMENT MEASURES cont.

Ten Possible Methods to Test What I Know about Media and Technology

1. List and define ten different terms related to media and technology.

2. Construct a set of short answer or multiple choice questions about media and technology that you could answer.

3. Record five possible questions for the answer: "Internet."

4. List ten interesting and relevant facts that you have learned from your study of media and technology.

5. Discuss a problem or "hot topic" related to media and technology in no more than three comprehensive paragraphs.

6. Construct a two-level outline of concepts you could explain related to your study of media and technology.

7. Summarize everything you know about an important media or technology concept you have learned.

8. Write a brief "how to" explanation for using a piece of computer hardware or software with which you are familiar.

9. Construct a rubric of skills and concepts you have examined during your study of media and technology. Use it to rate what you know or don't know well.

10. Design a comprehensive lesson plan to "show off" what you know about an important media or technology concept learned as part of this unit of study.

JOURNAL-WRITING TASKS BASED ON MYTHS RELATED TO TECHNOLOGY

DIRECTIONS: Summarize your thoughts for each of the perceived myths about technology listed below. Use each summary as a starter for a journal page to be written at a later time.

MYTH NUMBER ONE

Because we live in a digitized world, we are losing our "humanness" and our need for human touch.

_____

_____

MYTH NUMBER TWO

The information highway will result in most people doing their work from home in so-called "electronic cottages."

_____

_____

MYTH NUMBER THREE

Technology reduces learning and knowledge to information that is limited to hard-core facts, databases, and statistics eliminating opinions, feelings, and personal thoughts.

_____

_____

MYTH NUMBER FOUR

Teachers resist learning and using new technologies in the classroom because they are intimidated by their power and by their potential to put teachers out of work.

_____

_____

MYTH NUMBER FIVE

In another twenty-five years, technology will have replaced professional positions in our society to the extent that most pre-professional educational programs will be totally unnecessary, causing many university programs to become extinct.

_____

_____

JOURNAL-WRITING TASKS BASED ON MYTHS RELATED TO MEDIA

DIRECTIONS: Summarize your thoughts for each of the perceived myths about technology listed below. Use each summary as a "starter" for a journal page to be written at a later time.

MYTH NUMBER ONE
With the increase in media coverage of world and local news, newspapers of all types will soon become extinct. As with the dinosaurs, people living 2000 years from now will speculate as to what "really" happened to the newspapers.

MYTH NUMBER TWO
All home movies or personally filmed travelogues are boring to people not actually captured on film, so they are not of real value other than to the film's originators.

MYTH NUMBER THREE
As people of all ages depend more and more on video, radio, TV, and film for education and entertainment, book sales will continually decrease and consequently so will world literacy.

MYTH NUMBER FOUR
The growing tendency of people in many countries of the world to watch world class sporting events on television (especially on wide screen televisions) is causing a decline in attendance at real live competitive sports performances and will eventually influence the economics of sports from high school football games to the world Olympics.

MYTH NUMBER FIVE
The "couch potato" syndrome of excessive dependency on TV, resulting in people neglecting exercise, abandoning social activities, and ignoring family communication, is spreading and is a threat to family solidarity, community involvement, and overall growth in healthful living.

©1997 by Incentive Publications, Inc., Nashville, TN.
Media & Technology

BUILD YOUR OWN MULTIMEDIA TECHNOLOGY REFERENCE BANK

DIRECTIONS

Compile a fact or reference bank of these important multimedia technology terms using a separate file card for each item. Be prepared to add to it as the school year continues.

A is for **artificial intelligence.**
B is for **bandwidth.**
C is for **chip.**
D is for **disk.**
E is for **expansion board.**
F is for **flatbed scanner.**
G is for **grid.**
H is for **hacker.**
I is for **information superhighway.**
J is for **joystick.**
K is for **keyboard.**
L is for **loop.**
M is for **modem.**
N is for **networks.**
O is for **output.**
P is for **public domain.**
Q is for **queue.**
R is for **random access.**
S is for **spreadsheet.**
T is for **text search and retrieval.**
U is for **user interface.**
V is for **videoconferencing.**
W is for **windows.**
X is for **eXamples of software.**
Y is for **yeah computers.**
Z is for **zoom.**

©1997 by Incentive Publications, Inc., Nashville, TN.
Media & Technology

USING INVESTIGATION CARDS TO SMUGGLE THINKING SKILLS INTO CLASSROOM INSTRUCTION

Investigation Cards provide a tool for differentiating instruction in a classroom of diverse abilities, interests, and cultures. The cards are designed around Bloom's Taxonomy of Cognitive Development, with tasks written for each of the six levels. This makes Investigation Cards helpful in "smuggling" thinking skills into the curriculum.

Investigation Cards can be used in several ways:

1. Teachers can assign cards to students, or students can select their own cards.

2. Teachers can require students to complete at least one card at each level of the taxonomy.

3. Teachers can also assign Investigation Cards to cooperative learning groups, with each group having the same set of cards, or each group working on a different set.

4. Finally, Investigation Cards make excellent homework assignments, enrichment assignments, or assignments for students with special needs.

You will need a supply of blank 4" x 6" file cards to prepare the Investigation Cards. Create graphic cards for the activity. Cut the cards on the dotted lines and paste each one on the back of one of the 4" x 6" file cards. Then make a copy of each page of task cards, cut apart the cards on the dotted lines, and paste each task card on the back of the appropriate graphic card. If time permits, color the graphics and laminate the set of Investigation Cards for extended use. If time is limited, you may make copies of the task cards alone, cut them apart, and give each student or group of students the paper task cards for immediate use.

Note: The Investigation Card format may easily be adapted to topics such as computers, cameras, audio- or videotapes, and CD-ROM.

INVESTIGATION CARDS cont.

KNOWLEDGE

1. Record the name and publisher of your favorite video game.

2. Make a list of characters and the physical descriptions for each character in this game.

3. Write down the different obstacles and challenges for the player to overcome in this game.

INVESTIGATION CARDS

©1997 by Incentive Publications, Inc., Nashville, TN.

COMPREHENSION

1. In your own words, summarize the major goals to accomplish in this game.

2. Describe how you feel when you are playing this game.

3. Explain what special skills are required for being successful in this game.

INVESTIGATION CARDS

©1997 by Incentive Publications, Inc., Nashville, TN.

Media & Technology

INVESTIGATION CARDS cont.

APPLICATION

1. Compose a letter to the publisher of this game, telling why you like it so well.

2. Time yourself and a group of friends or family members playing this game. Determine who has the best time in mastering the game.

3. Construct a drawing to show a favorite excerpt from this game.

INVESTIGATION CARDS

ANALYSIS

1. Conclude why people love to play the different kinds of video games.

2. Deduce how publishers dream up the challenges and obstacles for video games.

3. Compare and contrast your favorite video game with one of a different title.

INVESTIGATION CARDS

INVESTIGATION CARDS cont.

ANALYSIS

1. Create a mini-poster promoting the purchase of this game by other kids in your class.

2. Think up a title and a set of challenges for a new game like this one.

3. Design a postage stamp commemorating the video game craze.

INVESTIGATION CARDS

EVALUATION

1. Criticize America's obsession with video games.

2. Rank order a set of alternative activities that someone could do instead of of playing video games in his or her spare time.

3. Defend this position: Video games develop their players' hand/eye coordination.

INVESTIGATION CARDS

©1997 by Incentive Publications, Inc., Nashville, TN.
Media & Technology